Pantalla Parade

Pantalla Parade

Laura Swart

PHOTOGRAPHY BY MITCH KERN

ALSO BY LAURA SWART

Ransomed

Blackbird Calling

Remember Also Me

Copyright © 2022 by Laura Swart
Pantalla Parade

Published 2022 by Sea Crow Press
Barnstable, MA
www.seacrowpress.com

All rights reserved.

No part of this book may be reproduced in any form or by any electronic or mechanical means, including information storage and retrieval systems, without written permission from the author, except for the use of brief quotations in a book review.

First Edition Trade Paperback ISBN: 979-8-9850080-7-4
Ebook ISBN: 979-8-9865676-0-0
Library of Congress Control Number: 2022941426

Cover Design by Mary Petiet
Cover Image iStock.com | Torsak Susma
Interior Design by Mary Petiet

The first man, Adam, became a living being; the last Adam became a life-giving spirit.
—*1 Corinthians 15:45*

CANTO 1

IDA

(THE CANTOR)

Air quality today is ten percent.
Smoke from the northern wildfires is mingling with the river mist and
getting in my teeth like the gnats of Exodus. There's a dip in the river,
there where the Indians used to cross on their way to the rodeo—
Dante's boiling brook of blood thinning out for ghosts on horses, and
river rocks moving beneath the strange weight of the hooves.

The sun tumbles over itself
like a stone caught in a current, and the river swallows up its banks.
Songbirds hold their songs, shorebirds are still, blue heron waits.
They all wait. Wait in the breezes, the coming mutiny in their wings.
I can't see what the sky is carrying, but the birds see it from far off:
they see wheat fields with black crows dotting the horizon.

I walk beside the river on Pantalla Street
and pass Marlow's Tea Garden. The paraders come here first, to the
Garden's iron gates and narrow stairwell, to painted plates on white
walls and Monet shelves with jade plants, to teacups and garden

tools, flowers and empty bird cages, dangling lights, metal tables and chairs, old dressers, and old, old floors.

The meaning of Marlow is *driftwood*—
wood floating on water, a ship deviating from course or being driven —or drifting, like a parade drifting into disturbing connotations: passivity, listlessness, violent insanity, mad, frenzied fury. From the Latin and the Irish come other connotations, though—to blow, inspire, spiritually arouse; a seer, a poet.

Frida's Mexican restaurant
is beside Marlow's. My bench is there, out in front. I sit and watch the parade, wait for my first interview. I, Cantor of Pantalla, will conduct interviews with the street's merchants and after the parade, will sing the liturgy of the street: of the merchants, their old wounds and new; and of the paraders, their flutes and feathers and costumes, their weapons of war. I will make them hear, make them feel, and above all, make them see. That is all, and it is everything.* I will sing —mouthfuls of music in the sentient breezes—and they will listen, because the song is of them.

There's no marshaling
of Pantalla Parade—no division of labor, no distinction between actors and spectators, no choreography, no instructions about where to gather or when to fall into procession. Pantalla Parade is a disembodied spirit with power in the collective, in its emergent properties. All have stepped onto the stage to interrupt, to cut off, to occupy the center of civic authority: the Street.

It's a play in motion, a soliloquy moving
through space, interrogating the common and the routine. Each parader wears a mask—a pantalla, a disguise, an illusion—and the masks, with their flourish of colors and feathers and beads, are tethered to faces with strings.

Inside Frida's,
servers flutter around their tables like wanton sparrows. Simón is serving outside today; he stands beside his station with nachos and guacamole and pitchers of virgin margaritas. He gives the people small samples, chips and guacamole on paper plates and imitation tequila in paper cups. Simón is named after Simon Peter, the one who tried to walk on water but couldn't bear the strange weight of belief.

His curls are piled up on his head
and he winks at the people and he's tactile and he's effeminate. These are the watermarks. I can't sing about them because words and expression and *thinking* that don't conform with the metanarrative are, of course, forbidden, egregious, sinful. Even in a parade.

And then Rembrandt comes along,
and Rembrandt paints a God who is both male and female, divine Father grasping his beloved prodigal with a man hand and a woman hand. A man hand and a woman hand! Like a paeony—*a paeony,* with masculine motifs of lions and tigers and dragons and the blood of warriors—but with *nymphs* hiding in its petals!

Frida closes up the patio
to keep the smoke out, and Simón moves his station inside. I slip in behind him, sit at a rosewood table with blue tiles, and wait for our interview. On the walls are crosses—large, rough, wooden crosses, dainty crosses with turquoise beads, and lurid, gaudy crosses. There are paintings, too, of women, Picassolike, half flesh and half skeleton, alive and dead all at once. Juxtapositions everywhere, like in Mexico—but maybe not. Maybe it's all perfectly sane.

Simón comes over with guacamole and chips.
Kisses me on the cheek and sits. I, like the beggar in Abraham's bosom, want to dip my finger in the waters and cool his tongue—

because I *long* for him; I long for his story, long to sing his liturgy. He dips a chip in the guacamole and eats all of it but a small piece, which he places on a napkin. Soon a little pile of chip pieces accumulates on the napkin. I take one and eat it. "*No, no, no, no, no!* Germs!" he says. I take another. He's seated close to a skeletal woman, unmoving, framed in dead black.

SIMÓN

In my childhood, always, I had my ears.
My ears, they were 180 degrees. It was very bad.
My teeth—very bad too.
Separated, one over the other.
That was hard. All the bullying I got.
Airplane, Dumbo.
So I worked very, very hard.
I save money, I paid for my surgery.
And after the surgery, braces.
And my life was like dark, then dark and bright.
For me, was like the butterfly. I, I can't describe.
The security, the confidence.
You know, the attention of the people.
All the girls—all the *girls*—like, I'm more attractive, beauty—
but beauty depends, you know.

What should be beauty?

Because I, I was in the closet.
Like, I always knew it. I knew it.
Like, when did you know you were straight?
You always know. Because when you are a child,
you know it, but you are innocent.
You, you don't think about that, even though you know.
You know who you are when you are a child.
But, society, all the jokes people do.
The jokes that make you keep your secret.
Ahh, gay people! Ha, ha, ha!
Everyone make fun—you don't want to be that.

You don't want to be that!

I already had the jokes: *Dumbo! Airplane!*
I don't need a cherry on top! *Si!*

So I came out slowly.
Because your friends don't know you are gay,
so it start to be a big, big stone in your arms.
A heavy stone.
I start to tell my friends, slowly, you know, one by one.

And then—my family open a restaurant.

Rice and beans, tortillas.
And I became a server. It was very, very good.
My dad, when I came home at 2 a.m. in the morning
after work, he was waiting for me.
He cook dinner. He was very lovely.
He covered the love side of my life.
You know, like cooking, cleaning, taking the dogs out.
Always joking, clapping, singing, dancing on the street.
When I was child, that make me so embarrassed.
But now? I love it. Like, thank you daddy for that,
because he break the rules. He break the rules.
So beautiful. Yes, oh yes.

Always my mom, she cook tamales and she sell.

She always very hard worked,
always was like, bzzzz, a bee. A worker bee.
She—*matriarca*. How you say that in English?
This suffering mom who gave everything to the kids.
You grow up with the mom, mom, mom, mom.
You know, the female, the mothers and grandmothers
is super important; the mom has control of the family.
You go to the school, come back, mommy's cooking.
You eat, you grow up with the *mom, mom, mom*.
The image of the mom, the grandmother,
is untouchable. Untouchable.

The restaurant was close to the train station.

At the train station, you see all the people on the train,
trying to go through Mexico into United States,
because no jobs. No jobs, no food. All the people
come from Guatemala, Venezuela, Honduras.
They stay in refugee camps, like spider web on the borders
on Mexican side of the States. Is kind of the States but not.
Is a territory who is now the land of no one.
Matamoros, who is in Tamaulipas,
is on the border, a border city.

Super dangerous for everyone. For everyone.

The bad guys come from the cartel,
and all these people, innocent, all these people
go on the floor, people running.
The guns—chucka chucka chucka—
the cartels block avenues
and they come in the morning for people.
If you are there, on the imaginary line,
you go in the car and somebody comes with a gun,
Give me the car! Or kidnapping.
And that can happen anywhere.
More in some areas, but can be anywhere.

All these boiling situations in the border cities,

I think everything start from many, many, many years ago.
Mexican government, you know, they create
poor people, poor people, poor people.
And when you don't have opportunities,
and then a guy or a girl told you,
Hey, you know, you want to make money?

So you have a micro, micro business,
and then they become these huge cartels.

They start to take the country.

And all these countries,
like Guatemala, Venezuela, Honduras,
they are—hard time. No jobs. No jobs, no food.
A lot of people are racist with small countries
like El Salvador or Guatemala or Venezuela, Honduras—
but not Argentina. Not Argentina.
Because Argentinian are more white.
Blue white people.

We're back to that, right?

When you see indigenous people,
you treat them like shit.
In Spanish, we say, wow! Their traditions!
The Aztecs—we, we almost cry, like wow,
I'm so proud of them, of their traditions, indigenous.
But if you are more white, *oh yes*!
You have much more opportunities.
If you look super indigenous, people is like, *ugh*.
Because who was the servers to the Spanish people?
The indigenous.

And the people on the train saying, *Can you help me?*

And when the train come, all these womans,
mothers and grandmothers, they cook.
Everyday huge, huge amount of food.
All these woman, they cook all day.
They give bags with food, and they *no* do it for they self.

Nobody paying nothing.
All these woman cooks, nobody helps
—not the government—
all these woman cooks.

And they just *serve*.

Because nobody wants to move from their country,
you know? Like, *nobody*.
They want to stay with the family;
they want to stay with their jobs.
Why you want to move and work like a crazy,
completely alone in this new world?
And then, of course you grow up with this idea,
Ohhh, North America! Amazing!
You can get whatever you want!
I think the world grow up like that.
But, nooo. You have to work very, *very* hard.
Is not that easy.

Is not that easy!

When I first came, the culture, it was shocking.
You know sometimes in the elevator,
full elevator—boop! Open the door,
I say good morning, nobody answer.
And no English. So like for me was hard.
The first couple months was very, very hard.
Very hard. And then, of course, winter.
The first winter, I like it, but it's like, Oh my God!
Oh no, no, no, no! It was, ahhh! I dunno how explain.
But those people who come from Africa or Middle East,
with different letters even, like no abcd?
Like oh my God.

Good *luck!*

The first time here, lots of tears.
But is not like I want to go back to Mexico.
No, no, no. You just adapt.
Adapt yourself to the situation.
The loneliness I live. Even all the time I'm around people
but I'm lonely. I miss all that connection,
the strongness of my family, all the food.
The people go on the trains, you know,
they are on top of the train,
jeopardizing their life. And for me is the same.
People screaming, *Go back to your country, Borat.*
A lot of people, *Ha, ha, you look like Borat!*
That happening here. Still.

But I'm a server.

I know it. I always know it, like a child knows. Server.
It's in my life always—restaurants. I always around that,
and I love. I love people and I love food,
and I like you feel comfortable.
You come to my restaurant and I treat you with respect.
I keep your table clean.
I know the perfect doses—when to talk, when to leave.
I like you feel happy. Comfortable.
I am careful, very careful,
because maybe you never go out—you never go out—
and is the only chance you have.
You have this money and you want to have nice experience.

And I give you plates of food, like womans at the train.

IDA
(THE CANTOR)

Pantalla de humo can be translated as *smokescreen*.
On Pantalla Street, even the buildings are pretending. The old Parish Hall, borrowed Baroque in sandstone with a false-front, is now a ballet company. The House of Israel, built in 1929 to house the Hebrew school, the synagogue, the Jewish community—lost its arches in a 1949 renovation, then was abandoned and left vacant, then was renovated, enlarged, and converted into condos chic and fresh.

There used to be strings of little houses on Pantalla.
Now, there is
Rajdoot Indian restaurant
Yann Haute patisserie
Mercato Italian Market
Wurst Uberkitchen
Asian street food
Kamal's Middle Eastern food
a Brasserie—dark and hopping
a ramen bar
Burger Inn with fish, elk, ostrich, chicken

liquor and wine and weed
Riverside General Store
Purr Petite, clothes for kids
a brow studio
Body Sugaring Boutique
Rodeo Smoke Shop.

The old movie theater still stands;
they're turning it into a popup waffle place. Next to it is Henry's Laundromat, then the pinball arcade, then the Chinese grocer, Ghan Vat Lan. Vat Lan sells only pop and smokes and candy now, like a road sign pointing away from itself. She's scooping M&M's into little brown bags when I arrive. She passes me a bag of yellows, violets, browns, greens—reds, even—resuscitated ten years after the red-dye scare, when public panic went wild and florid and red M&M's, containing no Red Dye No. 2 at all, were replaced with orange—a false-front, an indicator that truth is never a *given*; it is a coup, an intervention, an undertaking, a seminal craving.

We finger the candies,
Vat Lan and I. We look out the window and watch the paraders angle along the street, their fabrics and feathers held in Pantalla's surface tension like dry flies before their descent. Above the street, river geese are roosting in Osprey's nest. I send up a silent prayer: Get rid of them. They don't belong. Squatters. Vat Lan nods in silent affirmation, then begins her story. As she speaks, I think of Osprey. His lineage, his history, even his winter migrations are far off, incomprehensible—but he always returns, his wings wide over the river, shaping the afternoon light and spreading over everything the fragrance of wild grasses.

VAT LAN

my dad wasn't educated
he ran a grocery store
all of our friends were in the grocery store business
or they had a laundromat
or they had a restaurant.

these were the key professions
of the Chinese immigrants
who escaped communism
they didn't want to stay in China
they didn't want to stay!
the communists didn't like that.

my mom had all this fancy jewelry
you know, the Asian jewelry
the gold
and she knew the communists would come
so she hid it in a broom
put it in a bag and hid it in a broom.

she met my dad through a family member
they married, an arranged marriage
and he brought her over
to Canada
moved her into a bungalow with my grandmother.

nine months to the day, almost
my sister was born
then I came along a year later
then more sisters
my grandmother pretty much raised us
because my parents were always working at the store.

when I was old enough
grade one, grade two—
before I was tall enough
to look over the counter
and when I could read and understand
what the pop bottles said

I would, on Saturdays
go and work at the grocery store
from ten till ten
people would bring back
their empty glass pop bottles
and get a deposit for them.

the bottles would pile up
and I would sort them
take them to the back of the store
into this little attic
dirty with spider webs
I hated it in there.

7up goes here, Pepsi there, Coke here
then during the week
the different companies would come
take their bottles
wash them, reuse them
and restock us for pop.

later I stocked shelves
with cigarettes and candy
I dusted, bagged groceries
and when I grew, then
oh boy, it was great!
I learned the cash register!

Saturday was the busiest day
it was always my day
at dinner time my parents went home
and my sister and I looked after the store
we knew everything about how to run the store:
stock the shelves, do the cash, lock up at night.

as I got older, I realized I was missing out
Saturdays, my friends went swimming
or their parents took them to the zoo
or they'd go for a picnic
we never did that
Saturday was the busiest day at the store.

people in the neighborhood would come in
and do their big shop
my dad was a butcher as well as a grocer
so he would come in at nine or ten
on a Thursday night
and butcher a half cow.

he had a butcher block with a huge table
where he cut the side of a cow
he turned on the saw, this huge saw
and it would buzz loudly
and with his fingers
he'd push the meat through.

he had a meat grinder, too
to grind hamburger
he pushed the meat through
with his fingers
and a big drill like a screwdriver
would grind the meat.

sometimes my cousin ground the meat
she turned on the grinder
and with her fingers
pushed the meat through
and the big drill ground the meat
and pushed it out.

one time, my sisters
were fooling around
they were fooling around
not paying attention
and all my cousin's fingers
went through that grinder.

cute girl
really cute Asian girl
long dark hair
white skin
fingerless hand
behind her back.

my dad wanted a boy
we had seven girls
seven.
my dad gave us numbers:
number 2 daughter! number 4!
he always said

go to university
be a doctor or a lawyer
or an accountant or a dentist
so I can show all my friends
so I can save face
because I don't have a boy.

sometimes I think
why didn't you take us for who we are?
you have girls. why do you need a boy?
but it was lineage
there was nobody to carry on the name
and the boys took care of the elders.

once I heard my mom call him a name
a derogatory name that meant
you have no males
that cut to the bone
but now the boys go and the girls
care for their mother and father.

just think!
if one of us had been a boy
the others wouldn't exist!
even now
even now
that is the source of conflict.

when I started grade one, I knew no English
I spoke Taishanese
the language of my grandma
there weren't many Asians in our grade
a boy and twin girls half-white
with long braided hair.

I wore hand-me-downs
and a China chop:
hair cut straight across the bangs
down, and straight across the bottom
bowl cut, every two weeks
as short as possible.

I wanted long hair like the twins
but I looked like the little
Chinese boy at the back
chinky chinky chinaman, the kids sang
I hate the word *chink*
even now.

we never took lunches to school
we always ate at home
I remember one dish my grandma cooked
dry salted fish, steamed and pungent
and when friends came over, they'd say
what is that *smell?*

we always had smells like that
my dad would bring home
rabbits and turtles
we all thought they were pets
until they ended up on the
dinner table.

my grandma was old country
she slaughtered chickens in our backyard
she would bend their heads back
tie up their feet, slice their throats
drain the blood
that drew the kids like a magnet.

dead piles of chickens
and neighbors squawking
you cannot do that!
so she moved into the shed, closed the door
and we'd hear the chickens and the turtles
thrown into buckets of boiling water.

nobody else did that!
everybody bought chickens from the store!
why couldn't *we* buy chickens from the store?
my sister wouldn't eat any; she said they were dirty
she wanted store-bought chicken
wrapped in plastic.

in high school my mom made us go to Chinese school
I went for maybe a year or two
then quit
I hated it
that's when I started saying, *no!*
I don't want to know *anything* about the culture!

I know I'm Asian
but I'm gonna speak English
I don't want to know about my lineage
it's not important!
so I don't have a lot of the culture
I can't speak Cantonese.

but I can speak Taishanese
we spoke it at home; it's the dialect I grew up with
we spoke it with my grandmother
because it was the only language she spoke
Taishanese from the southern part of Guangdong
and now that I'm older, it's nice to know.

IDA

(THE CANTOR)

There's a fourplex on a little side street
behind the Chinese grocer, tucked away from the parade. Sloped roof
with a parking pad out back. Nothing to look at, really—except this.
On the parking pad are four garden boxes with dark soil surging at
the edges. Adolescent boys from the nearby detention home are
planting seeds with Dana, the local gardener. It's part of a community-service program to keep kids out of prison. I step gingerly into
the lineup of boys and we bend over the boxes, forgetting for a short
time our fragmented lives—Fentanyl scabs, indifference, innocence
lost. A swallow pivots in a corner of the sky and we strain to hear its
lyric, because there's nothing of the river's thrashing in it.

Dana, soft as a wheat field
and smelling vaguely of sweetgrass, hovers over one box, then flutters
like a sparrow to another. She's teaching us about indigenous ways of
growing food with the Three Sisters: corn, beans, and squash. The
corn stem emerges first, then the bean whorls around it, then delicata
squash spreads its wings and shelters the soil, shading out the weeds.
The boxes are divided into square feet. Each square can hold three

sisters, or sixteen carrots, or four bush potatoes, or nine onions, or sixteen radishes, or one eggplant, or four heads of lettuce. It's an imaginary grid, all of it tilled with blueblack fingers and the weight of so much suffering. Yet in Dana's stories, there's a promise of completeness, the possibility of wholeness.

DANA

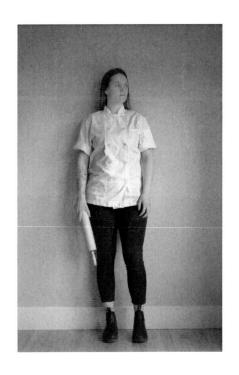

I was already a red seal baker
when I started my internship
at Eigensinn Farm and Hai Sai Restaurant
near Sing Hampton in Ontario.
Dad drove me out in my Nissan Juke
he crammed into that little car with me
and I got to hang out with just him
for five days.
Hey Dad, what does your tattoo mean?
How did you and mom meet?
What's your favorite Harry Potter movie?
I'd never thought to ask before.

My dad is Metis.
His grandma Rita knows our history
but doesn't talk about it.
For her, being Metis isn't something to be proud of.
She's from that time, you know.
I think it comes from the preconceptions
about indigenous people.
On government documents
Metis people are called
half-blood:
dirty
not French
not indigenous
you don't belong; you don't fit in.

When we arrived at Eigensinn Farm
we learned that I'd be staying in a weird little cabin
in the woods, a kilometer away from the house.
No electricity, no water
no windowpane

just a big hole in the wall
and a door that didn't lock.
We learned that I'd be working 100-hour weeks
with no pay
and I'd rarely be leaving the farm.
It didn't matter that I knew how to make
sourdough bread and croissants and puff pastry
because we'd be farming and butchering pigs.
That didn't sit well with my dad.
This is sketchy!
I don't want to leave my youngest daughter here!
But I was just so excited
to be there
to work hard
to get right to it.

We grew all the food we served
raised and butchered pigs, sheep, ducks, chickens, geese
and peacocks, too.
We were open three nights a week
and served eight to twelve guests per night.
$350.00 per person for an eight-course dinner
wine not included.
It was a whole experience for people to
drive the two hours from Toronto
to come and dine with us.
I would cook the dinner with my chef jacket on—
consommé
with small raviolis
served in
hollowed-out squashes
with holes drilled
in the tops

and flowers in the holes,
flowers with
long stems
that brushed
our guests' faces
when we served them.
wine bottles
turned over
with sorbet
in the indentations.
piglet barbequed
on an open fire.
potatoes carrots mushrooms.
petit fours
served on slender antlers:
truffles
cream puffs
almond squares
shortbread pastry
with chewy toffee
on top.

Then I took the chef jacket off
put on an apron over the fancy
polka dot dress
I bought at the thrift store—
and hot from kitchen adrenalin
stood behind the curtained doorway
smoothed my hair
stilled my heartbeat, my trembling hands
and served
every crease in my hands
still stained from the day's chores of
farming

butchering
hauling rocks
chopping down trees
building stages
for live performances and festivals and
creating mosaics and sculptures
with smashed wine bottles.
I got to see all sides of fine dining
starting in the kitchen at the beginning of the day
then seeing it through until the last guest left.
That was important to me:
all hands on deck for everything.
But the long hours
without pay and
the heavy labor
burned me out—
and crushed my parents.

After my internship at the farm
it was hard to go back to pastry school.
I didn't like being pigeonholed into
making wedding cakes
or chocolate showpieces or chewy macarons
it was just so impractical to me.
I liked making wholesome food
things from the earth
simple things done well
like growing vegetables—
it doesn't get more straightforward than that.
Or making sourdough bread
for me, bread
I just feel it so deeply
flour and water
so beautiful

so traditional
the sustenance of a nation.
You pull it out of the oven and
it crackles in the air
I just love that!
I love thinking about people throughout
history sharing a warm loaf of bread.
I never think about people sharing
a croissant or a danish
it's always, always bread.

I finished school and went to
Margaree Forks in Cape Breton for six months of
small-scale organic veggie farming.
I made one phone call
and the farmer Peter was like
Yeah, I guess you can come.
I had never met him before
and didn't know anybody in Cape Breton.
So this time when my dad drove me
he was diligent in dropping me off:
I'm going to sit down with your boss
We're going to talk about your work conditions
I'm going to make sure your room is okay
I'm going to drink a glass of the water there
And make sure everything's alright.

For one month Peter didn't say a word to me
not *good morning,* not *here's what we're doing for the day.*
I felt so lost
so isolated
but I didn't want to give up.
Communication got better once things started growing.
We had three acres of every vegetable under the sun:

we grew haruki turnips—beautiful, delicate, white—
a little like radishes, but soft and tender;
we grew bok choy
beans
peas
beets
swiss chard
broccoli
cabbage;
we planted fruit and nut trees
hazelnut
tomatoes
and corn
lots of corn—
and it was supposed to be so beautiful
all those corn stalks
but when we went to harvest it
every single ear of corn had been eaten.
Crows.
Everybody said
Yeah, that's the price you pay.
You know, like you had such a beautiful year
everything else turned out really nicely
that's just nature's tax.
And that's how I see the world
you give a little; you get a little
you can't get stressed about what's been lost
you just move on.

In my last week at Margaree Forks
a hurricane came through.
it was October, Thanksgiving.
Everything was bountiful
and the storm was coming in

and it was raining bad.
Peter said, *Let's go look at the garden.*
The garden road was washed away
and the garden was flooded.
We had to think.
What's our first priority?
What can we save?
What makes the most sense?
The hurricane was coming.
We pulled in all the squash
because it stores the best
everything else we would have to replant.
The storm clouds rolled in
and we raced down the driveway
and hauled in all that squash.
I remember what Peter said after everything flooded:
It will sort itself out, he said
in two or three days, it will sort itself out.

Later, after I left
bigger storms came in
Americans with big gin distilleries.
Tourism.
I don't blame them
it's such a special place
but it breaks my heart to pieces.
And now, when I think of Margaree Forks
there where the river runs along the edge of the garden
and you listen to the birds while you work
and everybody waves when you drive down the road
oh, it just makes me so happy!

So my dad, he builds motorcycles.
That's his passion. He started the shop

when we were young. There's family photos
of my sister Cassidy and I watching cartoons
and my dad building a motorcycle
in the living room.
Cassidy and I started our own small business
when I was eight.
We named our business RefreshWorx
we got T shirts printed and business cards
bought pop from Coca Cola, got two vending machines
put one in dad's shop and one in his friend's.
Picture this: a little kid visiting your business saying
Hello, my name is Dana Lee
I'm here to sell you a vending machine.
My entrepreneur mom taught us how to
introduce ourselves
shake hands, stand tall
ask the right questions
be professional, be taken seriously.

I started my own business when I was ten
a baking business called 7 Course Desserts.
I had spring pastry parties
and invited all my dad's friends from the shop.
Big heavily tattooed guys with leather vests
at a spring pastry party.
I baked for days prior—
mini cupcakes
little cinnamon buns
zippy lemon bars.
I wore a high ponytail and a white sundress.
My parents bought aprons, a floppy chef hat
and designed a logo with my big toothy grin
and a crossed whisk and spatula.
It was so sweet

all these adults eating my pastries
so supportive of what I wanted to do.
I know now how important it is
to foster someone's dream.

I used to dream of having a bakery
that I could ride my bike to
and my family would come
and get cupcakes from me.
Now I dream about growing vegetables
for people I care about
showing up on their doorsteps
with all these vegetables I've grown.

But maybe it's even bigger than that.
When I volunteer at the Boys and Girls Club
and see the kids learning
how to grow carrots for the first time
it brings the issue closer to my heart.
It's so good for hurting people to be outside
working on a project.
I want high-quality, delicious food
to be accessible to low-income families.
But how do I do that without a farm?
How can I commit to going into debt?
It just seems so unattainable
I can't fathom how I'd ever make that happen.

When I was farming in Ontario
I'd be getting yelled at
by the chef all morning, and I'd think
*Okay. I'm just going to weed the garden
hang out by the pond with the ducks.*
I think that's got to be my starting point—

farming my backyard
using food as a vehicle for love
and remembering Peter's words after everything flooded:
It will sort itself out.
It will all sort itself out.

IDA

(THE CANTOR)

Ahmed's salon
is kitty corner to Dana's garden, and he's promised me a free haircut with the interview. I wander over, soil still impacted in the creases of my hands. There are three chairs in the salon and a bald spot where the fourth should be. A high ceiling fan wobbles around an oblong circuit, girded by white walls that cloud over sometimes, depending on the light, like Lebanon did and Syria did, Ahmed says, when colonists carved them up and clung to them like hairs do.

I have a curly head of hair,
so Ahmed says he has to build up a cylinder by constructing corners at the top of the hair and keeping things elongated. "What that does, is it allows the curls to pile up and to be weighty around the crown of your head. After the crest of the head, the head curves up and in, so you really need that weight to build up. Otherwise, you're gonna have a flat shape."

One time I went to a different salon.
I sat in the chair and the stylist just stood back, hands pocketed,

waited for me to organize myself. Didn't say a word. Ahmed is different; he doesn't just stand there with no social skills. He says, "Hi Ida, how are you? Let me take your coat, show you where to sit. Would you be more comfortable putting on a smock? Come this way; let me lead you to the smocks and the bathroom where you can change. Can I offer you a beverage? It looks like you got a bit of a tan—did you enjoy your week?"

He knows bloody well
where the tan is from. He knows I stand on Pantalla Street every Saturday and sing its headlines, its scandals and politics. "I had a great week," I say. "Okay, cool. Hey, let's talk about your hair real quick. I have some great ideas about what we can do for the summertime. I have a couple of photos on my ipad that I want to run by you." He doesn't talk to me in the mirror; he turns me around and faces me, pulls up a stool and talks at eye level. "I'm gonna make you a bit of a bright red." "Sounds good." I disappear into my notes: I have a liturgy to recite in five hours.

A woman bustles in with her son.
"My son got a *horrible* haircut at First Choice!" she announces. "Look at it! They tapered the sides, and now the top is too curly. He looks awful. Can you help him out? He's going to his grade nine grad tonight!" The boy looks like a little old lady. Ahmed says to him, "What do *you* think?" "It doesn't look good." "Obviously it doesn't look good."

"I would love it if you could keep his curls
for the grad photos," says the mom. Then she walks outside to talk on the phone. Ahmed says to the boy, "I think you look like shit. I think we should just cut this short. Start fresh. Short and clean. It'll just have to grow out. How do you feel about that?"
"Yeah. Whatever."

Ahmed does the cut while my colour sets,
and when the mom returns, she's livid, flapping like a mallard taking off from the river. "What have you done to my son! This is *not* what I wanted!" "I realize that," says Ahmed, "but I had to salvage what I could. I want him to look good for his grad. I'm not gonna send him away looking like a little old lady with a perm set."

"He is *not* your son! It is *not* your head of hair!"
"Well you know what, I thought I had some creative license. Why don't you go outside and finish up with your call, and I'll deal with this." She stomps out, and he says to the kid, "Are you okay?" "Yeah. Sorry about that." "Are you pissed off at me?" "No. You did what you had to do." Ahmed shows him how to style it and even gives him some hair products.

The mom comes back in.
"What are we gonna do about payment?" "If you're not happy with the cut, I won't accept your money. You can thank me later when your kid starts getting compliments on his hair. Like I'm doing you a favor; your kid looked like shit, like an eighty-eight-year-old Polish woman." The woman's jaw drops. I hear a clicking sound. Then she looks me up and down, looks at my earth-stained hands. "What kind of place is this, anyway?"

AHMED

So you know you take nine months of school
And you think you're good
And then you get into the real world
And you realize there's more to this than you thought
So you get into taking further education
New York city, ivy league academies of hair training
And you really hone your skills.

And what you learn is the geometry of hair
Using geometrical shapes, breaking it down into a science
Physically changing what someone's face looks like
By manipulating their hair
A guy grows a beard cuz he has no chin
You sculpt his beard, and it looks like he has a chiseled jawline
A woman comes in looking tattered and worn
And leaves looking fifteen years younger.

The head and hair shape, one relates to another
It has to do with symmetry, with geometry of a face
It's the way you part the hair
The way you lay the hair down
The way hair falls on a human head
Down and back behind the ears
You take a few hairs here, a few there, and you leave a few
If it means grazing off a ½ mm, you do it
You cut it so it lays properly forward
Because that's the God-given way that it wants to grow
You can't really fight that.

It's like the Middle East
When the Europeans divvied it all up
Geometric shapes
Cutting things up, trying to force things
The Brits had a hand in Palestine (which they messed up)

The French had Syria
They divided it, made Lebanon a country
Why? Ski resorts, beaches; real estate, natural gas
Why would they do this?
Simple
Keep the people dumb and divided.

At one point the Arabs said to the Europeans
We don't want to be divided
We want to have a greater Arabian state
They shut that down pretty quick
Turned Sunnis and Shia against each other
Deep down inside we don't give a shit
You do you and I'll do me
But it's the white man that creates divide
What better way to dip your fingers in a country
Than to rescue it?
Do you think there were problems in Iraq
Before the US went there?
No
The US "liberated" them—but look how liberated they are now
Maybe you had to rule that country with an iron fist
We don't know.

Iraqis had free post-secondary education
University for free
Saddam knew (and I'm not saying he was a great guy
The guy was a piece of shit) but he knew
That an educated people is a powerful people
They were one of the few places in the world
With a hundred percent literacy rate
What was the tradeoff?
Don't badmouth the government
And that was just something they respected

All this is being provided—don't bite the hand that feeds you.

(And for some reason they were one of the few
Places in the world that was rat free
Saddam put signs up
Rats will be beheaded
Rats will get mustard gas.)

My parents grew up in the Middle East, in Lebanon
They left when they were young
Left the farm, five dollars a day—
Can't live on that
And they came
We grew up in a white neighborhood, white school
Just me and two East Indian kids
And you're the one bringing the stinky lunch
And the other kids are like, *What the hell is that?*
And you're like, *This is just my food*
You stink like garlic. What are those, cigars?
No, they're grape leaves.

And I was fat
So you're fat, you've got a different name
Your religious beliefs are different
The way you act is different—you're different
I was envious of the white kids
They were so well off
I was this abomination
They called me Paki—and I'm not even that dark
Their parents were educated, spoke perfect English
Could read and write
My parents didn't even finish elementary school
They could barely spell.

I was envious when I went to friends' houses
Their families were interactive and playful
At our house, it was dad the drill sergeant
Don't talk to me! You're just a kid!
Why are we discussing this? It's my way!
I always thought, wow, it would be so great to be normal
Look, his mom's sitting down with him
Helping him with his math
I really wished I had that
Now that I look back, it's kinda messed up
That I thought some white kid epitomized normality.

One time, my friend Cameron and I had a science project
And needed to do some research
So we went to his house
His dad asked him to clean up his room
And Cameron swore at him, slammed the door shut
His dad said, *We're gonna have a talk after*
About why you shouldn't act like that
Later I said, *You're gonna get a beating, aren't you?*
He looked at me and said, *No! Why?*
And right away I thought, Oops, said too much
Nope, this kid does not get hit.

When Cameron came to my house
We could hear my parents from my room:
Why the hell would you put blackberries in a salad?
What the hell is wrong with you?
It's just a salad! It was on the Food Network!
Dad left the dinner table pissed off
Cameron said, *What a crazy domestic dispute!*
Why are your parents yelling and arguing?
I said, *I don't think they're yelling*
That's just how we talk

They're just talking about salad; what's the big deal?
It's very much tradition, right? Why would you not put
Olive oil, lemon juice, and green peppers in your salad?
Why would you not make it this way?
Why the hell would you put in blackberries?

It was so embarrassing when my parents
Had to come to my school
Man, put me in a corner of the room
I remember we had this project for parents to come and see
Parents had to guess which project was their child's
I said to my mom, *Which one do you think is mine?*
She said, *Would you hurry the hell up and tell me which one is yours*
So I can look at it and we can go?
Your school is here to teach you; I'm not.

All the white kids went camping
One time I worked up the courage to ask my dad
I'm like, *Dad, can we go camping?*
And he goes, *What for?*
Well, everyone does it
And you know what his answer was?
Why would I go back to that?
He started laughing like I was an idiot
They worked the fields in Lebanon
So when they were harvesting
They set up camp and they tented
And they lived out there until their crop was harvested
He's like, *Why the hell would I do that?*

We went to Lebanon when I was a teenager
To my parents, it wasn't a holiday; it was going back
Growing up, my mom lived in a 400-square-foot house
And they had nine kids

I asked her about a structure on the side of the house
She said, *Well, it's a barn*
Why do you have a barn on the side of your house?
She looked at me like I was an idiot
Where else are we supposed to get our food?
So you just used it for animals?
No, the boys slept there in the summer
Where else are these kids going to sleep in a 400-square-foot house?

My mom was a great cook; I miss that
She cooked with soul, do you know
She said anyone who enjoys eating and has an interest in cooking
Is usually a good cook
We never had toast for breakfast
We had thick yogurt, olives, tea, veggies
Nice and light and fresh
For supper we had traditional Lebanese food
Kafta, tabbouleh, fattoush, lots of rice
Mom always said, *Eat eat eat eat*
Because in the back of her mind she was thinking
This isn't going to last
This isn't going to last long
We had a freezer full of food
Always, we had a freezer full of food
But they had nothing growing up
And what if we fall on rough times again?

I'm very appreciative of what my parents did
I respect them a lot
They were not perfect human beings
But I would not be here without them
Dad had me when he was almost forty; he was this old guy
Other kids would be playing with their parents
And my dad would be napping on the couch and always sore

Maybe now it's common to be a youthful fifty
But back then—maybe it's the culture—he was an old man
How did I know? How did I know what my dad went through?
His own dad left them when they were kids
And my dad's probably thinking
I'm here, you little shit
Be happy that you have a dad that's here.

The way things fall
The way they grow
The way they lay down
It's the God-given way
You can't really fight that.

IDA

(THE CANTOR)

I'm sitting in the chair surfing—
Ahmed has these tablets with preloaded magazines. I'm not actually *writing* my liturgy; I'm conducting market research, finding out what appeals to the masses. When I look up, I'm a bright copper red with curls piled up like Simón's. I gasp. "Trust me," Ahmed says. "I'm not gonna make you look bad." I sit for a moment, get used to the red. Then I gather my notes and join the parade.

The parade, distended with people,
moves through communal spaces, pushing past the funeral home, the hospital and the butcher, and arriving at the chapel on the hill with the three crosses and prayer labyrinth. No one stops there to negotiate things beyond—gathering, being, reverence, ritual, icons, the enduring and the perishing juxtaposed. Pantalla paraders want pageantry, not holiness; they want release from the ordinary, release from routine. They are like children at the mouth of the womb when there is no strength to deliver them.

There is singing coming from
inside the chapel, and piano, and melodies with dark-knit narrows. I leave the parade and step through a narrow aperture into incense and gilded saints, candles, pews, and prayers, folded hands, bent knees, and parted lips. A woman with lips red like a cock's comb and blue-black hair tight around her ears is sitting at the piano, leaning into it, touching the keys. Each sound, each lyric, each movement is a symbol bringing forth *more:* bringing forth transcendent Forms that like a wind shear find a clearing in me. And I tremble at the force of it.

MARIE

there was always a piano
and old movies of me up on the piano
not knowing how to play but close to it
the piano became my love
my lifeline
a place as a little girl where I could go
and nobody could take anything away from me
that's where I found peace in a home of chaos
I found a spot that was just for me

I could feel the ebb and flow of what I was playing
I got lost in the music

drama was a big part of my life, too
I think it was a way for me to escape
what was going on inside of me
when I was on the stage, the story came alive
it became my reality

drama fed my ego, my need for validation
but the piano was an extension of me

in the 70's, when I was just eighteen
I went to Oahu with my friend Amy
and we started singing there
busy clubs and big cabaret shows
Amy, she was super flirtatious, quite a bit older than me
and she would draw in these men
and these men said they would introduce me
to a big entertainer in Oahu
a mafia man
so I went backstage to meet him
walked into this room with a pool table
a huge Hawaiian man sitting in a chair

and a bed.
have a seat, he said

of course, the only place for me to sit was
on the bed
and I'm dressed up in a disco dress with a slit
so I sit on the bed and you know
the slit comes up
and I'm trying to be a big girl
what's your background where you from how old are you?
how badly do you want this?

it's the only thing I want to do
it's the only thing I've ever wanted to do

okay you know I have several clubs on the Island
how badly do you want it?
I want it bad
okay I'm just going to give you a scenario
I put you in a club and the manager
wants to sleep with you
it might just be a matter of five minutes

what would you do?
oh my God, no

you are young, aren't you?
anybody who has made it in this business
has done something to get there
it would be like putting makeup on or an outfit
you just put it on and you do it
and you get to do what you love
I paused for a moment
why don't you go think about it

'cause you won't get anything on this Island
if it's not through me

by that point I'd done a lot of stuff
drugs, alcohol, parties
lost my virginity to drug dealers
but this was not something I wanted to do
I can't do this, like there's just no way
like, oh my God
no.
so the meeting was set up and I said
you know what? I thought about it
and you can take your offer
and you can stick it where the sun don't shine
and he said, suit yourself
but you'll never work on this island again

that was the end
so I came home, I came home

I auditioned for a show at the Cove
they were doing a double show
a strip show
and a fast-paced musical family show
dancing and singing like the Osmonds
in amongst the strippers
those days were the flashdance days
leggings and a big top off the shoulder
and I always had good legs
so I auditioned: I sang and I did the dance
and the manager said great

I have to ask you to take off your sweatshirt
I took off my sweatshirt and he said okay

I made it
we toured Southeast Asia
we did the Supremes
the Andrew Sisters
Michael Jackson
we were pretty big stars, you know
money, TV shows, interviews, limousines
everywhere people screaming for autographs
and you know it was just kind of silly

this young pop group
thinking we were so grown up

I started working with all kinds of big bands
and going across North America
jazz clubs, the Banff Springs, Park Lodge
Whistler, Stage West
Kiki LaRue, Cape Ann, Klondike Kate
a funky children's theater group called Cats in the Attic
with a four-part harmony

theater in the day, singing at night
I was constantly *on*

it went on and on
I sang and sang
I had to do other things to support my music habit
I worked at a costume shop
worked for a trucking company
cleaned toilets
served tables—and I was good at that
because I was an entertainer
I could read people
and become what they needed

I would do anything for anybody
in order to be liked

but I always, always struggled
with depression and anxiety
there were times
when I wouldn't get out of bed all day
I couldn't even lift my head
but then I'd get up and put my makeup on
like the Hawaiian mafia man had said
put your makeup on and go and do it

so I would sing and oh!
my soul would come alive again

but woven into all my music
were my addictions
the drugs you know, the cocaine
people in the entertainment industry are just
let's face it, there's more addiction
a lot of us do it because we don't fit in
we're looking for something
we're insecure
we're drawn to the spotlight
the only place that feels normal

it's escape
it's fantasy

but it's not reality
how people see you when you're on stage
they see their perception of you
and you manage that perception
on stage I was in control

but I was always searching
always looking for something
always trying to heal
crystals, psychics, channeling

it was so awful
so dark

it opened me up to a lot of stuff
because as a child
I was one of those types that took everything in
oh my God I would see spirits when I was little
like a movie on my wall
cowboys and Indians coming at me to kill me
little girl in a bunk bed scared shitless
someone always lurking
listening to my thoughts
that realm is real!

everything changed
when I joined a recovery band

we played in an old church in the evenings
and we sang for the broken
come as you are
it doesn't matter it doesn't matter
just come as you are and let us love you
you know they'd come in and they'd be clean for awhile
then they'd go back out
then come back in

I would sing for the broken
and I fit in; I was home

because I knew broken
I knew it firsthand
I wasn't pretending to be someone else
all the masks for the shows
I didn't have to do that anymore
it didn't matter how skinny I was or how healthy
I could be me in this church I could be me
and sing for God and be his child

and that's what sparked me
that's when I started to heal

maybe I'm different you know
I feel highs and lows really deeply
that's who I am
I'd be a little girl playing the piano
with tears streaming down my face
it wasn't always bad tears you know
there was joy that I felt so deeply
but darkness got in there as well

when I was five I got the measles
and had to be isolated out in this trailer

and this man came out there
and molested me
you know there's evil out there
but I'm no longer a girl; I have peace
I don't think I could have gotten this peace
if it weren't for the other
my whole life has made me this person
and because of what I've lived, I can be with people

and I can sing for an audience of one.

CANTO 2

IDA

(THE CANTOR)

The mood of Pantalla is changing
like a goose emerging from the fog—first a slender neck, then wings.
Marie's music has brushed up against the paraders and reminded
them of their frailty, of things disappearing even as they press into
what is. These, afterall, are the sentiments of a parade: half flesh, half
skeleton; alive and dead all at once.

The paraders leave the chapel
and stumble upon one of Dana's boys asleep on the street just outside
the safe injection site—the shooting gallery, it's called. Come on in
and get your fix. We'll give you a needle and a juice box so you can
shoot up *out there* somewhere—maybe in the bathroom of that fine
dining establishment beside the river, the one that's going out of business because you are *everywhere* and you are violent and unpredictable and people are afraid of you. Then drink your juice and pass
out in Memorial Park across the street, there where the unforgotten
soldier is memorialized, the one who died for his country *out there
somewhere*—euthanized, just like you.

The boy is passed out and pissed up
and covered in scabs. Abigail, a counselor from the detention home, sits beside him, waiting for the dope team to come. She's quiet and watchful and her hair is like corn silk. I sit with Abigail and wait, but the dope team never arrives.

ABIGAIL

Always my mom was the staple.
She worked all day, then came home
and prepared after-school snacks and dinner
then went to her night shift
came home in the morning
made us breakfast
and went back to work.

Dad worked wherever he could
sometimes he worked out of town
and wasn't home for weeks.
We watched Criminal Minds together, he and I
and Law and Order
that was our thing; that's how we bonded
that's when he gave me life lessons:
Abigail, you gotta be happy
Abigail, you know I'm so proud of you.
'Cause he never had anyone
no one ever loved him
his parents didn't buy him clothes
so he wore girl clothes growing up
started drinking at twelve.
Abigail, you gotta be happy
Abigail, you know I'm so proud of you.
I never wanted those heavy conversations
but now that I'm older I can reflect
now that I'm older I can see.

Growing up, I didn't think it was weird
that some nights my dad didn't come home
and mom put us in the car at midnight
and we drove around looking for him.
We thought it was fun riding around
listening to music at night.

Growing up, I didn't think it was weird
that Dad asked us for money
or stole from our piggy banks to get alcohol.
We called my mom at work
Mom! What do we do?
Hide the alcohol, she'd say, and take the keys.
When I was in grade eleven, he tried to kill himself
down by the waterfall close to the train tracks.
He'd gotten drunk and wandered down there
and I just remember bawling
running down the tracks, trying to find him.
Abigail, you gotta be happy
Abigail, you know I'm so proud of you.

That was our reality, that was normal
that is still normal, even after I've moved
to a different city, made a home of my own.
Last year, Mom asked if he could stay with me.
Yeah, of course Dad can stay here—
but I have rules: no drinking.
He'll be working, she said. He'll be fine.
But his job never started
so he was here for three weeks, not working
and he drank
and I worried.
I couldn't leave him
he was capable of killing himself
and I couldn't be responsible for that.
One night I went up for a bath
and when I came downstairs, he was
sitting outside listening to the radio, drunk.

So I left him there
grabbed the car keys and hid them.

I knew everything I needed to do.
It was late, so I went to bed.
Then I heard a big thump
he had fallen off his chair onto the wooden deck
pitch black, music playing.
I turned off the music, tried to help him up.
He's my dad, right?
I tried to get him inside
tried to talk him down
but he didn't want to go to bed
didn't like being told what to do.
Who am I to tell him? I'm his daughter.
But he's old and he's fragile
and how could I leave him outside
curled up in a ball?
Abigail, you gotta be happy
Abigail, you know I'm so proud of you.

Just after I moved out here
my dad shut down
shut off
because my sister was raped.
We were at a house party
standing on the front lawn
and she was talking to this guy
super friendly guy.
I went into the house to get another drink
and when I came back, my sister was gone.
Text messages came, gibberish
then a snapchat: *help me*, it said.
I ran looking
found her on the street with no shoes on
bawling her eyes out.
I was raped! she cried.

She's always needed extra help
she exaggerates
she lies
puts herself in sketchy situations.
So I looked at her and I said
you better not be lying.
I still think about that
it still bothers me.

So the cops and medics came to the house
and my sister was in the bathroom puking
from shock
or alcohol
who knows?
I went to the hospital with her
waited all night, waited
for the sexual assault nurse to come
and get the rape kit done.
The *little lunch box,* they call it.
It's a tray of tools
they take pictures, swabs
look for bruising, grab marks
defensive wounds, scratches
little lunch box.
And that's something I still think about.

My sister she doesn't go to work now
she's on antidepressants, stress meds, heavy sleeping pills
she has nightmares.
During it all
I saw the mental health issues
and I knew I wanted to help people
with the effects of crime
help somebody to not offend

or help a victim regain their confidence
either one, because everyone has a story.
And that's how I started working at the detention home.
Abigail, you gotta be happy
Abigail, you know I'm so proud of you.

When kids first come to the detention home
they're scared and traumatized
alone in their room
they breakdown and cry
they're not in front of their friends
and they're fragile little kids again.
One-on-one they'll open up
tell you about their stuff.
All they want is to fit in, belong somewhere
have community, have family, be wanted
'cause their whole lives they weren't wanted.
Street kids especially
kicked out of businesses
kicked out of parks
kicked out of restrooms, all day long.
You're not welcome you're a nuisance you can't sleep here.
Nobody wants them
so they act like pieces of shit
they might as well act out and *really* be unwanted
'cause it's easier to self-impose than be rejected.

They're defiant, they have attitude
they're belligerent, they're rude
they have a pack mentality.
You tell one kid to do something
and he says *no*
makes it a scene
because all his buddies are watching.

He lashes out just to get that bit of attention
he starts fights, throws things, calls us names
barricades himself in his room
threatens the staff.
But he wants someone
he's testing you
does she care at all?

It's sad, some of the stories.
One girl was pimped out in Vegas
meth, fentanyl, living on the street.
She's fourteen; her boyfriend is forty-nine
and all we hear her say is
yeah, I can't wait to see him again.
That's her support, that's what she knows
that's her ride or die.
Another kid has severe fetal alcohol syndrome
he has the capacity of a five-year-old.
He was downtown with his older cousins
and they told him
beat up that man; take his wallet.
Do you think he knows what he did?
Get the youth to do the crime
they won't serve the time.
He has fits all the time
he is not well
did the cousins even think twice?
That's a human life
look at how it's being wasted!

Many kids in detention homes
earn their way there
assault
robbery

gangs
reckless driving
stolen vehicles.
They hate authority figures
hate law enforcement
have no regard for their crimes
don't follow directions
don't clean their rooms.
They've lived in disgusting places
so they don't care if they shit on the floor
or lie in their vomit
because that's their normal.
They yell at everyone
throw stuff, threaten people
brag about their crimes.

Then there's the mental health issues
once high-functioning kids, they are set off
by circumstances or bad drugs or who knows?
Psychosis takes over
they become vulgar, walk around naked
turn gray, lose weight.
Sometimes they soil themselves
and the whole house is laughing
they act like it doesn't bother them
but it does
and regardless of whether they did it on purpose
it's dehumanizing.
But it's a protective factor
if they're gross, nobody will touch them.

It's not like they're all coming
from the same kind of population.
Some come from good homes

and there's no excuses
but most have been abused
or sexually assaulted by people they've trusted:
family, parents, boyfriends, girlfriends.
Their parents are not in their lives
or their parents are dead
or their parents and siblings are in prison
entire families are involved in this stuff
it's all they know; they're born into crime
they start smoking drugs at eight or nine
commit petty crimes to support their addictions.
They have no regard for their life
they don't think they're valuable
they think they're pieces of shit
and they have nothing to live for.
That's why they do what they do
they'll always choose the high
despite the risks
a high is worth it every time
what else is there?

I'm not naive about these kids
but I give them a bit of self-worth
reflecting on good things
the times when they did it right
everyone can think of something
even in the worst situations.
And they'll tell me,
Yeah, I am really resilient
or yeah, I broke the law but look
I was able to feed my child because of it
I kept my child safe.
I try to set it up so they can see:
Like wow! Look at these survival skills you've attained!

Look how you've shifted your perspective on that situation!

Or you know, kids that have a lot of anxiety
and they're like, oh poor me
everything goes wrong for me.
I hate life
life is not worth living
everything goes wrong for me
I try so hard and nothing ever works out for me.
So I try to get them to reflect:
Tell me about a time when something good happened
or like, tell me about a time when you did something
and there was a positive result.
It takes two seconds to show them
that someone is paying attention
that there are people in authority who care.

But I'm not naïve; these kids throw stuff at us
these kids spit on us and threaten our safety.
So like at the end of the day
there is one goal: Go home safe
I want to go home safe.
But humanity—that's the main thing, right?
You can offer your humanity.
Look people in the eyes and say
I hope you have a good day.
Abigail, you gotta be happy
Abigail, you know I'm so proud of you.

IDA

(THE CANTOR)

I shiver like a crocus
under long snow as we sit with the boy, wait for the dope team to taxi him away. And then it begins. Quietly in a micro-moment. A police officer arrives. Leans in, squeezes the boy's shoulder. The boy awakes, unfurls, and like a wild animal, turns his horns on the officer. The paraders don't see it.

The boy thrashes like the river,
curses, howls, spits. The officer responds. Slams him face down into the street, knees him in the back and cuffs him. The paraders see it. A destructive narrative comes into being: *All police are bastards! APAB! APAB!* Tweet it, text it, snap it, film it. The crowd swells like a high wind and pushes in on the officer, some shouting one thing, some another, many not knowing why they are there. Tweet it, text it, snap it, film it. Don't think, don't investigate, don't question.

And now a photographer arrives,
his collar turned up against Pantalla. In his camera he holds the street —its breezes and odors, its buds and blossoms and clouds that wrinkle

up like a mudflat when the wind picks up. He holds pink skies and blue moons and crows that come in at night, hundreds of them moving en masse along the river, searching for that grove of trees with the bare branches, then settling in like black fruits ready to drop.

He holds it all—all of its ways and temperaments, all of its life—even as a revolution quivers before him. And the camera too quivers in his hesitant hands—because the boy, the paraders, the police—none of it is guileless; all of it is constructed, all levying, all clamoring, all impalpable as a wind. It is, all of it, *spiff*.

MITCH

you know I'm a photographer
I look through the lens and I construct images
that's what I do.
I produce experiences
lens-based, mediated experiences.

legend holds that the camera obscura was first noticed
under an oak tree by a Chinese philosopher
the branches and leaves created a subdued light chamber
and there was a hole in the canopy
and images were cast on the ground.

early churches also had subdued light chambers
clerestory windows, high up
with a narrow aperture for light to pass
and the light did pirouettes
it cast images on the walls, ceiling, floor.

then Leonardo started drawing
pictures of the world outside coming in
through the narrows
and the history of painting
was changed.

how do you render a three-dimensional world
on a two-dimensional surface?
you need an artist's hand
to trace those images
to transcribe that reality.

and the camera is quite like that in many ways.
it has light sensitive material inside
translucent material
that can interrupt the projected image

and create a surface for the image to be traced on.

early photographers retrofitted camera obscuras with
coated plates, the first light sensitive materials
then they started futzing with chemicals on the plates:
camera obscura could project an image
but what if the image could be captured in some way?

instead of the artist's hand tracing the image
the image would be captured
through the action of light alone
it would literally burn itself
into some kind of light sensitive plate where

the aperture would open, then close
and it would burn through.
and that is the dawn of photography; that is the birth—
the coming together of art and science
discovery and invention.

the human eye also is a subdued light chamber
you've got a hole
and the light comes in
and casts images inside your eye
upside down and backwards.

in the first year of life, you have this perceptual adaptation
where the brain rights the image
the brain and the body become acclimated
and in a slow process you start to see the world
right side up and forwards.

let me tell you my story
of perceptual adaptation.

I was born in 1965, New York City
raised on Long Island, went to PS #6 school
third child; older sister, older brother.

my father was born in Liverpool
adopted into a Jewish family in New York City
his blood was Jewish, but we were not Orthodox.
I hate to disappoint
but we were reformed Jews.

like so many other Jewish people
and especially New York Jews
we went to temple only for bar mitzvahs
and the occasional high holiday: Rosh Hashanah, Passover
we didn't celebrate, didn't study; I hate to disappoint.

we were gastronomic Jews
it was really just about the food
there's the gefilte fish, there's the chicken soup
there's the matzoh bri, there's the deli sandwiches
I guess I'm a bit of a disappointment to my rabbi.

my parents divorced when I was eleven
my brother went to live with my dad in Brooklyn
my sister moved to Manhattan
and I stayed with my mom.
we took an apartment in Queens

and I went from Long Island
to Queens:
tough, dense, multicultural, urban.
it was me and my mom against the world
and she used to sing that song to me.

(sometimes it seems like you and me against the world
when all the others turn their backs and walk away
you can count on me to stay)

I saw my dad on weekends
he took us to Chinatown
and we'd eat Yaka mein soup
and watch karate films
and play pool and play the horses at Belmont Park.

one day my mom pulled me aside and said
I'm gonna move to California
you can come with me
or you can stay here with your father
I was eleven.

I didn't even need to think about it
I was not going to leave my mom's side.
she told my dad we were going
on vacation to California
gosh, she broke the law!

so we drove in a 1975 Datsun Sunbird
with our dark tabby cat Carmen
from New York to Coldwater Canyon
did all the sites
Grand Canyon, petrified forest.

my mom and I moved every two years
I bounced around from school to school
in the San Fernando Valley
the kids were tough and bad:
gangs, drugs, alcohol.

I hit some turbulent waters
started running with some kids, getting into trouble.
when I was fourteen, mom met a guy
he wasn't a perfect guy, but he was good to me
he straightened me out and he took me off the streets.

then when I was eighteen my mom got lung cancer
and died.
Oh God I mean it was horrible
because it was me and her against the world, you know?
my mom used to sing that song to me.

(sometimes it seems like you and me against the world
when all the others turn their backs and walk away
you can count on me to stay)

I got a job in a camera store and
people would come into the store and they'd be like
well what should I buy
so I found myself in this kind of
ethical dilemma

should I sell this product that we mark up
giving me a little what they call *the spiff*
a little incentive to sell that product
or do I tell you about a better product
where I don't get a spiff

or do I go even further
and sell you this used thing
from the old days
which is a really cool thing you know
'cause it's got that older manual kind of appeal.

I always felt that dilemma was easy to navigate
I was much more interested in selling things I believed in
people would come in and ask my advice
'cause I would give the straight facts
and I started to develop a following.

now my sister had moved to Santa Fe
because she was an artist
she set up a nice little knitwear design company
and it was thriving
and she was always saying, come to Santa Fe.

I finally went
we got a studio together, 2,500 square feet
she was building her business
and I started working at the main camera store
and developing my practice as a photographer.

it was fantastic
I was having a great life
building my skills, building my portfolio
doing freelance photography
I was living large—friends, hiking, romance.

and then one night at four in the morning
I got a call
my sister had been in a car accident
guys drinking
big truck

lost control
crossed the yellow line
head injury
killed instantly.

when I went to the hospital, they said

you don't want to see
so I never looked I never even looked at her
and that was a very difficult time, you know
losing my mom was hard, but she was sick for a year
and I got to say goodbye.

but losing my sister instantly like that
worst thing in my life, because in a way
my sister took over for my mom
to love me and nurture me
she did that really well, too; she was very good at it.

(sometimes it seems like you and me against the world
when all the others turn their backs and walk away
you can count on me to stay)

so I was not in a good place after that
I needed a way out
so I did—I left Santa Fe
and I have some regrets about that
but I felt like I just couldn't take the pain.

I moved to North Texas, found a little apartment
took some journalism classes
started working for the local newspaper
did some freelancing, mad mainstream media photojournalism
started to heal and find myself again.

then one night I'm out at a bar called Cool Beans
and there's this girl there
and I think one of us challenged the other to game a pool
and we had some room-temperature Guinness beer

with a big foamy head on it. and we've been together ever since.

(sometimes it seems like you and me against the world
when all the others turn their backs and walk away
you can count on me to stay)

I went to grad school
started teaching
started exhibiting my work in professional galleries
then I got a teaching offer
from a little school in Louisiana.

we moved down there
like let's do it
let's go on an adventure
I don't know that I would have done it all the same way
but we did it and we had a wonderful time.

we moved down to Ruston
a little university town in Louisiana
I had a mix of kids in my classroom
and saw all the tension
and the racial divide.

there was literally a division
between the haves
and have nots
it was very clear
it was very stark.

but Oh my God it was the Deep South
wow, I mean so much southern hospitality
and good food
just like I'm a gastronomic Jew

I was also a gastronomic Southerner.

shrimp po'boy
étouffée
jambalaya.
you know there was a lot of racial tension
but we would cross the tracks

go over to the southern part of town
and there was this old black woman
who ran a lunch counter
out of her home
called the Blue Light.

she served up all the good food
the black-eyed peas
the fried chicken
the cornbread
there across the tracks.

so we spent three years in Louisiana, had a daughter
then moved to the Great White North
to a new teaching job
we sold our house, did a big garage sale
rented a u-haul, loaded up that truck, and drove to Calgary.

we crossed the border at Sweet Grass, Montana on one side
and Coutts, Alberta on the other side
and oh God what a great move
I'm so thrilled that I am not raising my daughter
in the Deep South

in an environment of racial tension
class warfare, crime, poverty, division.

look, I've lived in Baltimore
I've lived in New York, I've lived in L.A.
I've lived in seven cities in the States

and Calgary's my favorite
it's safe; it's got everything
I mean it's cold—it's cold and it's dark and I don't love the dark
but they say that the colder cities, the northern cities
are the happiest cities.

I don't know; I've definitely found some happiness here
we found a home with a little workshop
I do editorial and photojournalistic documentary work
I do some commercial photography
and of course teaching. often with the camera

you don't want to look down on the subject
you want to meet your subject at eye level.
so with my students, I try to get down a little lower
give them the confidence and support they need
to grow and blossom as the next generation

of artists, photographers, and designers.
I've always seen the camera as
a device to navigate social contracts
you sit down with someone and you say, you know
let's get to know each other a little

let's talk and do a portrait.
I'm looking for an image that will say something
in a different way
I try to tell a story
that touches on different topics

like race, class, gender, human identity.
I think storytelling has been at the heart of my work
meeting people, earning their trust
depicting them in a certain light
and not betraying that trust.

I feel lucky to have gone down this road
to be a storyteller
and the portraits have been telling my own story.
my mom, my sister
later on, my dad and my brother

all of these people are dead now
and I don't have access
to a lot of the details
I want to ask about.
but I look through the lens of my story

and I see light passing through the narrow aperture.
the light is doing pirouettes—
casting images on the walls and ceiling of my memories
and the world is right side up now
right side up and forward.

CANTO 3

IDA

(THE CANTOR)

One small spark—
a boy and an officer—and a fire is kindled. It moves up the street toward Pascal's Wager, my favorite brasserie on Pantalla. I sit outside with the staff and smoke. We lean into each other and talk about the parade, no stage faces.

Blaise the owner, Esther the cook, Adam the server.
They've worked together for decades. They're family. And when I dine at Pascal's Wager, I feel like I'm home. Adam quite often sits with the guests after his shift ends, listens to their stories. He's intelligent and thoughtful, well-read. People come and sit with him at the bar, and the night goes on. "Even the sea has limits," he says when they pour out their lament. "It can go so far and no further."

There's a room upstairs
above the dining area called the bird's nest. Blaise reserves it for small celebrations, and Esther prepares succulent dishes—soupe au potiron, tomates farcies, coq au vin, clafoutis aux poires. It's in some ways the command center—lights, music, a disco ball. You can't see

the disco ball from below, but its light moves all around the brasserie in a sort of subdued light chamber.

Sometimes the staff goes up
to the bird's nest to rest. It's like a lookout: they can see everything below, watch without partaking. On Parade Day, Adam by all accounts was feeling a little blue, a little anxious, so he drank some wine with us, ate a baguette, and fell asleep in the bird's nest.

ADAM

it was always there
from the time boys were noticing girls, I was noticing boys
it's not like I made a choice
or I can look at a trauma and say
that's when it started
it just sort of unfolded naturally
I came from this family of really strong women
and addicted men
family stories were always of women
courageously pushing on in spite of their husbands

so I had this sense that being male was morally inferior
and that created shame around my gender.

my dad was a drug addict
that was part of what made him remote
he was a fairly benevolent guy, but I never thought
he was all that interested in *me*
so I think there was a gap in my sense of who I was—
particularly around my masculinity
I didn't know what a real man looked like
I didn't know what it meant to be a man

I became desperate for any man to tell me I was okay
I wanted their approval; I wanted them to be my dad.

I kept my secret for five years
don't talk like that don't dress like that don't move like that
then I went to Bible school
and found students who were safe
I started telling people for the first time
and that was really good
the other students said, we don't know what it's like
we don't understand your experience

but we're willing to stay friends
we've got our own stuff we're dealing with

that felt pretty good
that was a good couple of years.

but I wanted a family
and after Bible school
I wandered in the wilderness for a while
I came to the city
went back in the closet
and met a woman
I told her on the third date—long enough to trust her
but not too late for her to pull out
she decided to go for it, and we got married
we had children, found ourselves a funky little church
and then I really went back in the closet
because like
what am I?
who am I?
how am I going to communicate that I'm gay?

and what's the point of that
now that I'm married to a woman?

the world changed quickly in just seven or eight years
it became a completely different place
I found that very difficult to deal with
not because society was changing
but because the Church was
our pastors came to me and said
we think your sexuality is a big part of who you are
we'd like to move from the traditional to the affirming position
and perform gay weddings

that threw me into huge crisis
how does this work now?

it must be true on some level
how do I figure that out?
how do I make my sexuality work for me?
how do I make it fit with marriage and children?
I didn't know what to do
we had all agreed:
this is what the Bible says
this is how things are
and I kind of bet my life on that
I had gotten married, had children
did what the Church told me to do
and now the Church was saying something different
and it felt like, maybe I'd made terrible choices

so I started to play with my identity as a gay man
made it a big part of my life— and our marriage was in trouble.

then I found a support group with traditional Christian views
they didn't talk about homosexuality at all
they rarely mentioned it
very quickly, I learned that I could tell these people anything
and nobody would judge me
because the stories were all out there
there was nothing I could say about
porn addiction, drug addiction, alcoholism
or anything else that would shock these people
my small group leader, a man, had slept with
thousands of men

until Jesus got hold of him
told him there was more.

so I began to speak up
and they said, God still loves you
he's still with you in those areas of pain
he wants to connect with you
how does that feel?
and we listened to God
we took our stuff to God and waited for him to speak
and that was life changing for me—
that God would speak to me—
so I thought, okay, I will stay married and stay with my family
even if I'm completely miserable for the rest of my life
I'm gay and there's no way I can be happy in this marriage

that was my expectation; that's where I was at
and I made a deal with God.

I said
I will do what you want me to do
as long as my wife is with me
but if you ever take her away from me
I'm gonna do my own thing
you're God, but if you stop doing what I want
my sexuality is in charge; my sexuality will take over
because if you take that away from me
I don't know who I am
God said
I want that deal

but your sexuality can't be in charge of your life
I've got to be in charge.

so I, I did it
I said yes
and at that moment

my relationship with Jesus completely changed
I had never had any meaningful experiences with Jesus
(I'd heard people at church say
Christianity isn't a religion
it's a relationship
they always say that
and it never meant anything to me
whatever, right?
I'm gonna gut it out because I think it's true
but it doesn't mean much to me
it's not a relationship
in relationships one person doesn't stay silent
for forty years)

in that moment everything changed for me
it was a true spiritual experience.

it felt like my heart was being ripped out
and a deep sense of emptiness was taken out of me
there was nothing left
I was hollow
and then just a few moments later
it felt as though Jesus filled up all those empty places
and he was with me—really with me

I felt him
I changed completely.

Augustine talks about the explosive power of God's love
once I experienced that love
the other stuff didn't seem so important
Jesus, whatever you're asking me to do
then I'm going to do it
because you seem fantastic

and being with you is better than anything else
even if I don't understand
I'm going to make the sacrifice
because things we sacrifice for, we value
if it costs me something, it must mean something
and it costs a lot

but it's worth it
because he's pulling for me.

my sexual orientation hasn't changed
I am still a gay man
but I have fallen in love with a woman
and when that happened
the attraction came along with it
and the intimacy we have cultivated is good
that is God's best for us
that is his vision of sexuality and marriage
and I would say
my life is better; my life is richer

but the Pride movement says, no
you're not one of us.

you don't talk like us don't dress like us don't move like us
yet 98% of LGBTQ don't want to be part of Pride
just leave us alone to live our lives
then there's this 2% out in front, in the media
they don't represent our community well
their activism is moving into the realm
of controlling people's thoughts
controlling the agenda beyond actual issues
they're over-reaching, and the community sees that
they're exercising power over the lives

of the people they claim to represent
they say, we're not here to police your sexual identity
we're not gonna say who's in and who's out
if you say you're in, you're in

it's a rhetoric of openness and diversity
but underneath is intellectual fascism—

a course of power that says
if your life doesn't look like *this*
you're not actually a gay person
if you don't believe *this* and if you don't do *that*
you're not one of us
we're sexual people
if you're not getting the kind of sex you want
you're not healthy
sexuality is fundamental to who you are
but gender? you can pick and choose your gender
move it around
so if you don't see gender as fluid, you're not one of us

I think we're in trouble
because we have that exactly the wrong way around.

if something as fundamental as gender is up for grabs
when you force people to choose *everything*
it produces incredible anxiety
we haven't even given people the tools to work through that
we just say, oh, you get to decide what gender you are
but I'm really stressed because
this seems like a really big choice
is anyone going to help me with this?
no, it's fine, just choose
you can't just rip that foundation out from under people

and say it's all fine
that creates all kinds of problems
when cultures start to blur the line between male and female
it's an indication of the decline of the culture

there's something about male and female together
that reflect God's image in a way that one gender cannot.

there are two phenomena in culture
that we're not distinguishing between
and that's getting us into trouble
there's gender dysphoria
and then there's rapid onset gender dysphoria
which in my mind is a cultural phenomenon
it's not a genuine clinical condition of gender dysphoria
suffering from that is like a trip to hell
they really suffer; they don't feel at home in their own body
it's overwhelming
they have profound shame at being the gender they are

it's almost a rejection of their birth sex
more than wanting to be the other sex.

one guy I know dresses as a woman for two hours a day
that's how he manages it
the breakthrough for him came when he stopped judging himself
instead of saying
it's a terrible thing I'm doing I hate myself for doing it but I just can't help myself
he started to say
this is something I need to do to get through my day and that's okay
that was huge for him—so freeing
he kept doing it after he was married
he tried to keep it from his wife, but you know

it's hard to hide something like that
she was unhappy about it for a long time
then she read some stuff and he read some stuff
and they had this conversation—
what if you just kinda let yourself off the hook?
obviously, she wasn't down with him doing it publicly
but what if you just let yourself and not shame yourself?
that was huge for him
the start of something really good in his life
and he started letting God love him
that's the task of the Christian life
like yeah, I do this
maybe Jesus is inviting me into something else

but right now he's with me in this thing
right now he's with me where I'm at.

we all have legitimate needs
and we've all met those needs in illegitimate ways
workaholic, drug addict, addicted to food
what is the need behind that compulsive behavior?
some say, I don't have compulsive behavior
that's fine
but can you see your need for love, your need for significance?
can you see how shame has come in and messed that up?
I think we all experience shame in some part of our lives
and Jesus so often comes in and says
I don't see you as somebody who should be ashamed
I want to free you from shame

I love you in those situations no matter what
I stand ready to meet your needs.

he never says, you should be ashamed

he never says that
he's amazing
he's patient and he's gentle and he walks with us
and he's inviting us into an abundant life
it's hard to hold that tension in place—
to go, yeah, I'm broken and there's lots going sideways
and I feel the shame
but God is on my side
inviting me into something more
more than I could ever imagine
and it costs a lot

but it's worth it
because he wants me.

IDA
(THE CANTOR)

One small spark
a boy and an officer. Pantalla Parade morphs into an unruly carnival, *the world standing on its head,* Bakhtin says. Blasphemy, parody, and profanity approved, legitimized, enacted, and celebrated. The crowd surges like a swell of blackbirds into Pascal's Wager, and the riverbed boils over like Dante's brook of blood. I stand still, liturgy in hand.

THE CANTOR'S LITURGY

See the mouse tracks in the dust along the river?
Tiny like wild bluebells, moving in small curves.
Then an erratic hare
then coyote prints—straight and deliberate.
Feel the power, the intention, the Mission
feel it strongly in the trees.
Mouse tracks, hare tracks, coyote tracks
moving along Pantalla Street
then crisscrossing at the safe injection site.

See the safe injection site
across from Memorial Park?
Sacred ground
with a flame always burning for the unforgotten soldier
and a fountain filled with needles.
Pantalla Parade ends *here*.

Police officer confronts a boy
boy unfurls, thrashes, spits

paraders don't see it.
Officer puts him in a half-mount
boy screams:
Get your hands off, you pig! You're hurting me!
Paraders see it—
tweet it, text it, snap it, film it.
A destructive narrative comes into being:
Defund the police! Fuck the police! All police are bastards!
Tweet it, text it, snap it, film it
don't think, don't investigate, don't question
a child will lead you.

Pantalla Parade morphs into a carnival
a stampede rushing towards a cliff.
The world stands on its head.
Rules, rituals, and reverence
are suspended
the sacred and profane merge into a parody.
The paraders are on stage now
reading a script, playing a part.
Raid the merchants!
Plunder their goods!
Steal their arms!
Arms from Ahmed: scissors and mirrors and distortions.
Arms from Dana: tomatoes and squash splashed in the street.
Arms from Vat Lan: brooms without treasures, bottles without necks.
Arms from Frida: smash the glasses, smash the plates
smash the skeletons already dead.

They push into Pascal's Wager
and seize forks and knives and coat racks.
Forks, knives, coat racks!
Pierce, cut off, occupy!

Adam bolts upright, wide awake;
he rushes down from the bird's nest and cries out

> "Quiet!
> Be still!
> You are like whitewashed tombs
> outwardly beautiful
> but inwardly full of dead people's bones!
> You clean the outside of the cup,
> but inside, it is full of greed and violence.
> You are the glory
> and the scandal
> of the universe!"**

The crowd becomes quiet
the crowd becomes still—
a solitary man has stepped in
stood among them
and become a fixed referent.
And they tremble at the force of it.

Adam steps up on a chair.

> "You who know so much, answer this," he cries:
> "Where were you when the earth's foundations were laid?
> Have you held the dust of the earth in a basket
> or weighed the mountains on the scales?
> Have you measured the waters in the hollow of your hand
> or with the breadth of your hand marked off the heavens?
> What is the way to the abode of light
> or the place where lightning is dispersed?
> Can you bind the twinkling of Pleiades
> or loose the cords of Orion?
> Tell me, if you know!

> Does the hawk take flight at your wisdom?
> Does the eagle soar at your command
> and build his nest on high?
> Did you give the horse his strength
> or clothe his neck with a flowing mane?
> Where does understanding dwell?
> Where can wisdom be found?

Adam steps down from the chair
and speaks in a still, small voice.
The crowd strains to hear and to see.

> "When you see a cloud rising in the west,
> immediately you say, 'It's going to rain,' and it does.
> And when the south wind blows, you say,
> 'It's going to be hot,' and it is.
> You know how to interpret the appearance of the earth
> and the sky. How is it that you don't know how to interpret
> this present time? Your greatness lies in your power of
> thought; therein lies your dignity and your merit.
> Let wisdom, not instinct, be your guide!"**

One by one
masks and
weapons fall
and rotate
like coins tossed in a potter's field.
The paraders turn on their heels
Osprey turns in the sky
and the river is smooth and bright.

All this time
Simón has been watching
listening

treasuring the words of Adam's mouth.
He wades into the river
there where the Indians used to cross
and the river rocks move beneath the strange weight
rubies and emeralds and sapphires
pirouetting like Pleiades
or like a rainbow.
Simón bends over, picks up a white stone
white like a wedding song
and the creases about his mouth
reach down
into the fertile memories of Pantalla Street,
the river clasping him like a mother might.

*Joseph Conrad
**Blaise Pascal, Matthew
***Job, Luke, Blaise Pascal

ACKNOWLEDGMENTS

My profound thanks go to Sergio Pelicans, Graeme Scott Lauber, Mitch Kern, Dana Lee, Omar Sleiman, Ghan Vat Lan, Marie Bridge, and Katie Jones for sharing your stories.

Mitch, thank you for your lovely, powerful photographs.

Dayla, thank you for our Mission lunches and talks; thank you for your sweet friendship.

Thank you to all the merchants of Mission who shared their stories and expertise.

Peter, thank you for helping with the transcribing and for your listening ear.

Anika, thank you for your expertise and your strong, caring support of others.

Jeff, as always, I love you; thank you for editing the manuscript.

Sea Crow Press and Mary Petiet, I am so grateful to you for taking this on; it's been a delight to work with you.

And lastly, my love and devotion to my Lord, the Second Adam.

ABOUT THE PRESS

Sea Crow Press is committed to amplifying voices that might otherwise go unheard. In a rapidly changing world, we believe the small press plays an essential part in contemporary arts as a community forum, a cultural reservoir, and an agent of change. We are international with a focus on our New England roots.

Sea Crow Press is named for a flock of five talkative crows you can find anywhere on the beach between Scudder Lane and Bone Hill Road in Barnstable Village on Cape Cod.

According to Norse legend, one-eyed Odin sent two crows out into the world so they could return and tell him its stories. If you sit and listen to the sea crows in Barnstable as they fly and roost and chatter, it's an easy legend to believe.

Manufactured by Amazon.ca
Acheson, AB